TAPE SUCKS:

Inside Data Domain,
A Silicon Valley Growth Story

by Frank Slootman

Dedication

To the men and women of Data Domain.

Contents

Introduction

Silicon Valley has been birthing renegade technology companies for the better part of a century. The storied lineage traces from Stanford's Fred Terman to the Varian brothers' Klystron amplifier, from the hallowed garage of Bill Hewlett and Dave Packard to the bold "traitorous eight" who fled Shockley Labs to form Fairchild Semiconductor. These companies, to be sure, broke new science and engineering ground—yet their most lasting legacy may well be their pioneering approach to business itself. They blazed a path that led to Intel, Apple, Oracle, Genentech, Gilead, Sun, Adobe, Cisco, Yahoo, eBay, Google, Salesforce, Facebook, Twitter, and many, many others.

What causes a fledgling company to break through and prosper? At the highest level, the blueprint is always the same: An upstart team with outsized ambition somehow possesses an uncanny ability to surpass customer expectations, upend whole industries, and topple incumbents. But how do they do it? If only we could observe the behaviors of such a company from the inside. If only we were granted a first-person perspective at a present-day Silicon Valley startup-cum-blockbuster. What might we learn? This document—the story of Data Domain's rise from zero to one billion dollars in revenue—is your invitation to find out.

For anyone curious about the process of new business formation, *Tape Sucks* offers a provocative, ripped-from-the-headlines case study. How does a new company bootstrap itself? What role does venture capital play? Why do customers and new recruits take a chance on a risky new player? Frank Slootman, who lived and breathed the Data Domain story for six years, offers here his clear-eyed, "first-person shooter" version of events. You're with him on the inside as he and his team navigate the tricky waters of launching a high-technology business. You'll feel—deep in your gut—the looming threat of outside combatants and the array of challenges that make mere survival an accomplishment. You'll catch a glimpse of an adrenalin-fueled place where victories are visceral, communication wide open, and esprit de corps palpable.

I first met Frank about ten years ago, when he was one of the new chieftains at Borland Software (a celebrated Silicon Valley firm that was under new management and retooling to become an enterprise software company). I was the CEO of a small, high-growth software startup that Borland was interested in acquiring. Borland wasn't the only company courting us about an acquisition, but in the end Frank was the most persuasive.

What you discover—usually within about thirty seconds of meeting him—is that Frank is direct and unafraid. What you learn over time is that he is also ambitious, full of integrity, action-oriented, a bit restless, intrinsically competitive, economically minded (meaning frugal but also facile with econometrics), athletic, and a wide reader and student of history. I used to enjoy observing Frank hold court in his office as he got pitched on the latest product or sales opportunity. He would wait patiently until the speaker's prepared remarks eventually tapered off and the real conversation could begin. Frank has an independent vision of the world that doesn't seek or especially seem to need outside endorsement, and he expects you to either conform to it or convince him where precisely his thinking might be unhooked. This can be a difficult task, but when it is accomplished, Frank reorients himself unreservedly and embraces the new frame.

Frank has put to paper here a detailed, candid accounting of Data Domain's trajectory as experienced by a principal. For some reason, when journalists, technology beat writers, or business historians write the story of a high-tech company, they tend to lapse into clichés, cobbling together uncritical news clippings and friendly interviews in a kind of luke-warm, assembly-line synthesis. No insight. No point of view. No soul or fire. As you will quickly sense, *Tape Sucks* is the opposite of such books: As an honest, informed perspective on technology wave riding, *Tape Sucks* allows you to observe things at close range and get an unvarnished picture of how it really worked for Data Domain.

The upshot is that the principles of the early entrepreneurs of Silicon Valley are alive and well. Their straightforward ideas include employee-ownership, tolerance for failure, unfettered meritocracy, faith in the

8

power of technology breakthroughs, a preference for handshakes and trust over contracts and lawsuits, pragmatism, egalitarianism, and a belief in the primacy of growth and reinvestment over dividends and outbound profits.

May the fresh, true story of Data Domain prompt you to "Go, and do likewise."

Eric Müller
Society of Kauffman Fellows
Palo Alto, California

TAPE SUCKS: *Inside Data Domain, A Silicon Valley Growth Story*
by Frank Slootman

I was CEO of Data Domain, Inc. from the summer of 2003 until its acquisition by EMC during the summer of 2009. At the time I joined, Data Domain had about 20 employees, no customers, no revenues, and a few units in field test. With a few million dollars left in the bank, we were months away from running out of money.

During the next six years, Data Domain grew to sell more than all its competitors combined. We broke the billion-dollar sales barrier in less than seven years, adding more than one thousand employees and six thousand enterprise customers worldwide. We were seen as the "eight hundred pound gorilla" in the space, but we sure did not start out that way.

Why write this?

Having been part of a recent successful venture, I regularly receive invitations to speak and consult with aspiring audiences. I find myself repeating observations, and wanted to produce a text that is better articulated than my always off-the-cuff commentaries and recollections. Also, with this source document, in-person discussions quickly accelerate past the basics and become more pointed, resulting in more productive exchanges.

Inevitably, there is also potential for business success stories to be so embellished over time that they become unrecognizable; when that happens, the learning becomes more the stuff of legend than history. By creating this time-stamped account while events are still fresh in my cache, I hope to check this natural drift toward aggrandizement for myself (and perhaps others as well).

My background

I still say I was born on the wrong continent. I immigrated to the US from my native Holland, the only "apple" that "fell" so far from the family tree. This society's premise of personal responsibility, individual liberty, and free enterprise stood in stark contrast to the Euro-style social welfare state of my youth. In America, everybody wanted to get ahead, entrepreneurship was celebrated, and people were born optimists. Where I came from, people seemed more resigned to their fate—personal success was frowned upon, even mistrusted. I held a long time fascination with America, and instantly felt more at home here than I ever had in my land of birth.

It was hard getting my first real job here in the US in the mid-1980s, as the economy was not good then, either. I recall IBM rejecting my application at least 10 times in different places. I wanted to work in tech, seeing it as the future, but my alien credentials didn't help.

I arrived here with an advanced degree in business and economics from the Netherlands School of Economics, Erasmus University Rotterdam. In contrast to the prevailing attitudes of the times, academia in Rotterdam was a business affair. I remember the faculty dean telling us new recruits on our first day of school, "we're here to crank out entrepreneurs!" I liked it! Since my graduation in 1985, they have repackaged the curriculum as RSM (for Rotterdam School of Management), and the school now has international acclaim and credentials—but in my day, nobody over here had heard of it.

I finally got my first job in the corporate planning department of Burroughs Corporation in Detroit, Michigan. Burroughs was one of the "BUNCH" (Burroughs-UNIVAC-NCR-Control Data-Honeywell) challenging IBM's hegemony. I was a staffer in a small planning unit attached to the executive offices to help analyze, plan, and prepare new initiatives. Our big project was the acquisition of Sperry Corporation in 1986, which formed Unisys. Remember the "Power of 2"? Our deal had one principal rationale: we're small, they (IBM) are big, so we need to get bigger. While size matters, size isn't everything—as Data Domain more recently proved in unmistakable terms.

It was a start, though I wasn't big on corporate staff jobs, and as soon as the opportunity arose I eagerly descended down into the trenches. Throughout my career, I worked in the crevice between technology and sales: monetizing technology and figuring out how to get to market and make the transition from technology to business.

Despite being consistently underestimated by large and small companies alike, the tech-market gap is wide and deep—finding ways across is the toughest challenge many businesses will face. Best sellers have been written about it (Geoffrey Moore's *Crossing The Chasm* is a deserved classic).

In the next stop on my way to Data Domain, Compuware provided a big career break. When they acquired a sizable company in the Netherlands and struggled to run it from Michigan, I was dispatched as the general manager of the division—for once, my Dutch credentials were helping matters along. I moved back to Europe with my family for a few years.

Moving on to California, I advanced up the product-management ranks at Borland, an attempt to resurrect the illustrious brand established by such landmark software products as Turbo Pascal. The company transitioned admirably from a Windows, indirect channels, "shrink-wrapped," low ASP (average sale price) operation to a Java, direct enterprise sales, high ASP business. As a public company, the board was challenged to communicate and manage expectations during the company's transition to a broader enterprise play that involved a comprehensive application-lifecycle management strategy. There was much pressure to live up to our steady near-term capital market expectations, while simultaneously investing in a new generation of products.

Borland faced hard choices and was constrained by its past performance, a pattern that influenced my views on how to navigate the capital markets with a publicly traded company. Pandering to short-term investor needs for rapid stock-price appreciation can hamstring the company longer term. Investors are in and out of stocks all the time—you cannot let the near-term pressures dictate your strategy.

My days with both Compuware and Borland were marked by a growing desire to get my hands free and run things the way I saw fit. While it didn't seem this way at the time, most of our daily energies were consumed with grinding our way through and around the "system" to deliver business impact—in other words, clearing internal hurdles and barriers. I had fire-in-the-belly, perhaps as much as my employers could stand.

Leaving Europe and coming to Silicon Valley in 1997 was more than a geographic relocation; it was a deliberate migration to a place renowned for its flexible, aggressive, anti-status-quo approach to business. I experienced a sea change in attitudes and it opened the door to the possibility of running a startup myself. Where you locate yourself is a huge factor—looking back on it, I wasted much time not coming to Silicon Valley sooner.

Data Domain

Data Domain invented a new class of data center storage that eliminated redundant data before it was written to disk. Inline, on-the-fly—it just worked. The technology came to be known as *data deduplication*. In the days before data deduplication, in certain data-storage applications such as the nightly backup, the same data was backed up night after night, creating massive data redundancy and a corresponding cost and complexity.

Data Domain delivered disk storage that achieved reduction ratios of 20:1, changing the relative economics of tape media (the historical choice for backup storage). People could now afford to use disk for backup instead of tape. Magnetic tape mostly exited with the onslaught of iPods, YouTube, etc., but in enterprise data centers there is still a ton of tape on the floor.

The balance of power had shifted decisively toward disk; our mission was to put tape out of existence. We knew that—if successful—Data Domain could re-invent a multibillion dollar market.

Data Domain consumed about $28M of net capital from its venture capitalist investors. Put differently, we needed that $28M infusion to get from inception to running the business cash positive. We went public on Nasdaq in 2007 (stock symbol: DDUP), and through a secondary offering later that year raised another $175M for a combined total of $300M. Being cash positive, we really didn't need the money for operations, but a strong balance sheet reassures enterprise customers so they buy gear from a small supplier.

Large enterprises are conservative and risk-averse—they like to buy from suppliers whose names have two (HP), three (IBM), or four (DELL) letters. This fear-based behavior can scarcely be overstated. Large enterprises consistently prioritize their buying decisions to minimize the risk of embarrassment backlash. Huge premiums are paid in the misguided name of "playing it safe." Dominant suppliers carefully cultivate and nurture this incumbent bias.

With that $28M of venture capital (VC), we realized a so-called "exit" or valuation of $2.4B seven years later. One of our main investors said that Data Domain—by itself—returned the entire venture fund back to its limited partners (LPs). LPs are the people who put up the capital of family foundations, university endowments, and other capital concentrations. This type of outsized capital multiplication is what VCs live for (that, and Google IPOs).

Format: Modular

The observations in this book are written without much structure, often summarily, headline style, or somewhat nonlinear. It is helpful to read from the beginning, but you can (for the most part) enter these pages at random. The mini-chapters can be consumed in minutes—see if there is a nugget in there, maybe try it on for size. Or read the whole thing on a plane flight, or wherever you do uninterrupted thinking.

Intended audiences are startup CEOs and anybody involved or interested in business startups. These are merely observations, not lessons learned; "lessons" implies a broader applicability, a pretense I wish to avoid. Every startup is different. Circumstances, timing, personalities, opportunities—few things repeat themselves.

There is power in looking at situations with the mind of a five-year-old child who has little to reference and no sense of limitation. As you will see, I found it beneficial to bring some people into the business fresh to the space, rather than relying solely on multi-decade veterans who were set in their ways, prisoners of their own experience. If even one or two observations here cause you to rethink what you're doing, I hope you will consider it worth the read.

Chapter 1
Nobody knew

People have told me that I somehow "knew" that Data Domain would become the blockbuster success it became. Let me dispel that impression. I wasn't that clairvoyant—nobody knew. We were one portfolio company out of hundreds, and expectations were muted.

"Data Domain" is kind of a funny name—you could actually find the words "data" and "domain" in a dictionary. In Silicon Valley, new ventures seem compelled to name companies with contortions of vowels and consonants that taken together are hard to pronounce and are not referenced anywhere (yet). People often assumed we had been around much longer because we had such a grown-up company name! How's that for marketing?

Why did I join? In the spring of 2003, there wasn't much to look at. Due diligence? Data Domain didn't even have their own offices yet. Customers? Zero. Financials? Just a steady burn of cash. The venture did have first-tier investors, which I thought compelling—not just the firms, but also the individual partners in those firms who staked their personal reputations on the company.

From the perspective of an operations guy, there is a lot of riff-raff in venture capital: posers, herd mentality, technology infatuation, too much education, not enough experience to appreciate what grit and focus it takes to grow a business out of nothing. To have a fighting chance, you want to be with the best firms, and the best partners in those firms. Odds are already exceedingly low for venture success. Said differently, you are hoping these guys are smarter than you are in sizing up the opportunity. Hope isn't much of a strategy, but so close to inception there is little else to hang your hat on.

The next thing to look at is the team behind the venture, and the Data Domain team looked hard-core to me. It seemed like more than half the company had PhDs in computer science. I figured this must be a hard problem, with such a talent concentration: top talent doesn't just show up for interesting problems, they come for hard problems. I'd bring down the average IQ of the company by joining, which felt right to me.

These guys were impressive. The principal founder, Dr. Kai Li, was a computer science professor on leave from Princeton who had decided to come out west. Kai set up shop as a so-called entrepreneur-in-residence (EIR) at New Enterprise Associates (NEA) on Sand Hill Road. NEA was to become one of Data Domain's founding investors, along with Greylock Partners. Kai's link into NEA was Forest Baskett, a partner at NEA and a significant force behind Data Domain in the embryonic days, staying connected with the company throughout the journey.

Hollywood's depictions of inventors aside, Kai did not have a blinding epiphany for Data Domain while standing in the shower one morning; he had time on his hands, wanted to start a company, but had no idea what it was to be about. Which goes to show that not all successful companies are conceived in divine moments of insight— some just start with a university sabbatical spent in a fertile setting like Silicon Valley.

A second founder joined Kai: Ben Zhu, who was an EIR at another venture firm, USVP. (Ironically, USVP ended up punting on a Data Domain investment; regrettable for them, but a reminder of how difficult it is—even for those closest at hand—to spot breakout potential). Where Kai was brilliant at the abstract and conceptual levels, Ben was a hard-core technologist. He brought the skills and perspectives of an implementer: he built stuff.

The third founder was Brian Biles, a veteran of SUN and VA Linux. Brian is a "pure sang" product management guru. He is the best at product management I have ever seen. This is an oft-lacking skill set in startups as well as within larger companies, and Brian's discipline and diligence in figuring out pricing and feature sets is unmatched in my experience. Brian was a bit of an unsung hero in a startup culture where technologists often rule in the early going. It didn't help that he had a truly soft-spoken, low-key delivery (we often joked that he sounded like an NPR reporter when pitching customers or investors). But Brian would go on to effectively lay waste to the competition, in his understated style, through sheer product management superiority.

It was unusual that none of the founders were data-storage folks. They all had systems backgrounds with specialties in things like parallel processing, supercomputing, and graphics—hard stuff, but not storage. In hindsight, it helped explain how some of our breakthroughs came about: they ended up betting on Moore's law, the microprocessor subsystem, and avoiding the entrenched bottlenecks in the storage subsystem (jokingly referred to by us as Seagate's law). Disk drives are notoriously slow compared to in-memory processing. Data Domain's landmark invention, data deduplication, is inherently lookup-intensive, as it has to reference every segment of data before the system decides that it either already has (or has not) stored an incoming chunk of data. Relying on disk for this determination, our founders decided, was a losing proposition—this direction ended up creating an ever-widening gulf of separation between Data Domain and our competition.

Data Domain's first true storage domain expert was Dr. Hugo Patterson, a PhD from CMU. Hugo became a quasi co-founder over the years, mostly indistinguishable from the actual founding team, carrying the title of Chief Architect and, later, Chief Technology Officer (CTO). He knew storage like few others, having spent many years at preeminent storage companies like Network. Hugo has probably forgotten more about storage than I have ever known.

While the company was conceived inside the walls of New Enterprise Associates' office, its second founding investor, Greylock Partners, further incubated Data Domain for the next year and a half. Data Domain moved out of the Greylock building in San Mateo and into its own space in Palo Alto the week I joined the company in 2003. NEA and Greylock shared the A-Series funding round. Aneel Bhusri, the Greylock investing partner, had been anointed as the company's first (interim) CEO and had been capably spurring the founding team forward until he passed the baton to me 18 months later. We brought in our third and final venture investor with Ron Bernal of Sutter Hill Ventures (SHV) when we raised the B-series in December 2003. Our final C-series round was done internally (meaning by our existing three venture investors) in 2005, led by Greylock Partners.

The problem Data Domain was solving—enabling disk economics for backup/recovery storage—spoke to me. In a prior life, I had been asked to restore years of email archives from tape in support of a discovery process in an IP lawsuit. What a nightmare! Tapes had been lost, or become unreadable. Slow, error prone. Just miserable; people were working around the clock in shifts. But tape was about 5x cheaper than disk, and this trumped all else.

With Data Domain's ability to neutralize that economic advantage (via 20:1 reduction ratios), I felt convinced the world would beat a path to our door—provided we could build it, integrate it, and scale it (no small feats). It is hard to examine every bit of data for repetition when it's coming at you like a fire hose, and I was merely scratching the surface of technical difficulty.

Would this idea really come together and captivate customers? Nobody knew. We, the people on the ground floor, were perhaps the most surprised by the extraordinary success we enjoyed. We often felt there was a form of providence at work, an invisible hand tracking our journey, guiding us—at times protecting us, even from ourselves.

Chapter 2
Creative destruction

If you registered the reference to Adam Smith's "invisible hand," you have probably also heard of "creative destruction." The famed Austrian economist Joseph Schumpeter is usually associated with this term, but the basic idea goes back all the way to the works of Karl Marx. The notion (which has experienced a recent resurgence via Clayton Christensen's writings on disruptive innovation) is that in order to create something, you have to destroy something else in the process.

This was true for Data Domain in a visceral way: we built our business on the ashes of the tape-automation industry. Mind you, we ignited the fires that torched the tape business—we attacked it and tore it down, one tape library at a time over a period of years. We declared open season on tape. Our first marketing slogan was "Tape Sucks, Move On." Not too subtle. We took creative destruction literally. The tape industry fought back with what they had, later shipping products that mimicked ours.

The point is that there is only so much money in an industry. Only the Fed can order up fresh cash from the printing presses—the rest of us have to take it from somebody else. It isn't a zero-sum game in a narrow sense: new industries can dramatically grow the size of the pie, but in the aggregate most economies only grow at small clips, fueled by population growth, trade, and productivity gains.

When you are a startup trying to sell a new product or service concept, you need a clear sense of where the money is coming from. Put differently, what is your intended customer *not* going to buy in order to make room for your product or service in his or her spending allocation? Who are you displacing and why?

As you start selling, you better have your pitch ready. People don't buy much because it is "cool" or "neat"—in the enterprise datacenter, people buy stuff that lowers their cost. Either achieve the same with less, or achieve better results at the same cost. There are cases when customers do go upstairs and beg for more money for a new project, but the bar is very high for them to even consider that kind of exposure to the brass.

Friction goes way up in the sales process. Even new services such as social media that were impossible to envision get their income from existing industries, attacking established problems in subtler, more powerful ways. Facebook and its social media peers are new media growing out of the ashes of old media.

So, creative destruction is an axiom of business: you are not going to grow much without exacting a proportional decrease in business somewhere else. You better know whose livelihood you're going to mess with.

Data Domain had the good sense to attack a product category that was not much short of loathed: tape automation was a hard-to-avoid evil because disk had been unaffordable for backup. If you thought disk was a medieval technology, tape was pre-historic.

A challenged product sector is obviously a much better starting point than attacking a category that is favorably regarded. When picking a fight, don't seek out the most formidable opponent.

Chapter 3
Do you know your technology use-case?

Data Domain was founded on re-engineering an existing IT workload, namely the nightly backup and recovery cycle, a specific operational discipline that every business undertakes on a 24-hour basis. That was good because we could sink our teeth into a real-life application problem that everybody has, one with budget and staff assigned to it that is monitored for operational effectiveness. We could study it, become experts at it, and learn how much we improved on the status quo with our new contraption. This became the basis for a credible go-to-market initiative that would succeed only to the extent that it resonated with the intended audience.

Many technologies are conceived without a clear, precise notion of the intended use. There is plenty of hoping and praying going on that some new technology will magically find a suitable problem to solve. Often, we think we know, vaguely, in the abstract—but the truth is we have no clarity on how our technology stacks up in that use-case, relative to alternatives.

This fundamental disconnect is often dismissively listed as a "go to market" problem: something to be figured out later. Well, figure it out now—if you haven't, you are relying on luck. Lousy bet.

In the storage industry, technologists have been forever intent on developing the mythical clustered file system that solves all the impediments and limitations of any storage system ever invented. The technological urge to build it fails to realize that any real storage system ends up having a design center that trades pros and cons in support of specific workloads and use cases.

There is no lack of startups that develop products, devoid of any application-specific intent, and proceed to hire a whole sales team to take their products to market. They accelerate their cash burn, often triggering a back-to-the-drawing board, re-start cycle—oops.

Start with the application or use case, not the technology. Don't make it an after-thought. Ass-backwards, it is awfully hard to successfully recover from a technology-led venture that cannot locate its target. Like an unguided missile, it will just burn itself out and splash down in oblivion.

Chapter 4
Snuggle up with your customers

Snuggling with customers sounds like baseball, motherhood, and apple-pie—hard to disagree with. Maybe so, but few ventures take this notion to the level needed. We decided early on at Data Domain that we were going to get our engineers, product managers, field engineers, and executives close to the customer, and let that customer voice guide our engineering and product priorities. We listened intently, discussing amongst ourselves to make sure we heard right. Before Data Domain received its first full round of funding, the founders had already received specific feedback from dozens of enterprise users about these specific product concepts.

Any other competing thoughts, proposals, or initiatives had to take a backseat to what we heard from our customers. That is harder—there are always tons of people inside the company, on the board, with ideas for you to consider. We always reverted back to our True North, the customer, which helped us focus, quiet the noise, and strengthen our resolve.

This focus is hard to maintain: a startup is like a combat zone, a very confusing, unstable, fledgling enterprise where you are "pushing a rope" half the time. Big companies are stable by their own inertia: it is hard to get them to change. A startup is the polar opposite, which is both a strength and a weakness—it wants to change all the time and there is little to keep it in a groove.

Ratcheting up customer focus assumes you are tuned in to a specific application or process. In the case of Data Domain, we received consistent and unmistakable messages back from our customers on what we had to do to improve their backup processes. We concentrated our resources on "making it so." If we got confused or lost our resolve, we would circle back and poll a cross-section of customers.

It is remarkable how little our strategy changed from dollar zero to a billion in sales. The most important thing we did throughout the journey: resist the ever-present temptation to muck with the strategy.

Another upside is that customer closeness benefits the sales process, because customers prefer vendors who really want to know them and learn their business. Higher levels of trust and respect develop in the relationship, which helps overcome the gravitational pull to want to buy from much larger competitors. If you're in the weeds, customers will let you know that, too, by the lack of traction you get. "Customer intimacy," popularized in a 1993 *Harvard Business Review* article, is a timeless idea.

Not every startup lends itself to such an intense customer focus: some new ventures are supply-led, not demand-inspired. Consumers could have never asked for an iPod until they actually saw one first. Our business was about incrementally improving an existing process, an example of straight-line innovation. We didn't propose to customers to do away with backup altogether, just the devices that they backed up to. We still worked within the confines of an existing process, which lent itself well to an intense customer focus.

Chapter 5
Drive your own revenues

Selling is heavy lifting—no way around it, it is hard. In startup thinking, there is always the lure of getting somebody else (preferably a heavyweight) to carry your bag. Some investors are likewise reluctant to invest precious startup funds on a direct sales and marketing build-out. And so, not surprisingly, the plan becomes: Step 1, try to land an OEM deal with Cisco or HP, and then Step 2, sit back watch the revenue roll in. Plus, the market endorsement from said big-name vendor is priceless marketing collateral. Sounds like a great plan, doesn't it?

Well, we didn't do it. To us, it seemed akin to selling your soul to the devil. First of all, you get divorced from your customer because the OEM is now between you and them, making customer intimacy challenging. Plus, as the OEM becomes a large part of your business, for all intents and purposes they basically own you without paying for the privilege. When they say, "jump," you are left with few answers other than "how high?" The longer it goes on, the more impossible it becomes to reverse. A worse scenario is one in which they actually sell very little, yet are driving your R&D agenda and tying up your scarce resources. Never forget that nobody wants to sell your product more than you do.

Our archenemy in the business was EMC (who eventually ended up acquiring Data Domain). They had sought an OEM deal with Data Domain a few years before but did a deal with a competitor instead. When they finally bought us, the competitor was discarded overnight—because EMC now owned us, they didn't need the OEM partner anymore. Ouch.

Deal economics also make the case against OEM deals: you end up getting 10-20 cents on the end-user dollar, or thereabouts. Even though you own the IP, they get the bulk of the revenue. I remember saying to prospective OEM partners that Data Domain would still be better off going it alone even if we ended up losing 8 out of 10 deals against them, so lousy were the terms of an OEM agreement. We would take those odds any day. EMC could not beat us with their OEM partner, and they were more or less forced into the bidding process for our company. Making yourself "scarce" is something to ponder.

What if EMC had been able to beat us with their chosen OEM partner? We simply didn't believe they had the technology to beat us, having encountered the OEM partner numerous times in the marketplace. Why did the other company do the deal with EMC on such dreadful terms? They must have thought it was the only way to beat Data Domain—they surely could not do it under their own power.

Building and scaling an effective sales and marketing organization is painstaking work that takes years.

Learning how to make a salesperson (a) effective and (b) economical, and then applying that to an increasing number of them requires a detailed, ongoing analysis of how that process works. You simply cannot invest intelligently in revenue generation if you do not understand how to ramp effectiveness and make the underlying economics work. It should be obvious that a sales force that loses money will only accelerate cash burn—in the absence of deep pockets, not a game to be played for very long.

There is great value in strong sales and marketing: you control your destiny, and you don't need anybody else to hit your numbers. If you have aspirations to go public, you cannot do so without a predictable model that you control. It is also a way to weaken competitors. At Data Domain we hired away the best of the best from our competitors—not only did we gather strength, we weakened them at the same time.

Ulysses S. Grant once said that victory is breaking the enemy's will to fight. Our version of victory was a great salesperson quitting the competition and joining our band of brothers. Breaking their will to fight (prompting "surrender") was one thing, but getting them to defect outright and rally to our cause—this was crushing for incumbent morale.

There is plenty of resistance in the venture world against building out a direct sales and marketing function because it is so costly. In this regard, we had one super-important thing going for us: high margins. Our product margins were north of 80%. The trade-offs are obviously different for products that struggle on the margin front.

Related to the affordability of a direct sales force, we took the view that the entire realm of marketing needed to be managed as a ramp for sales. Data Domain's VP of Marketing, Beth White ran marketing explicitly as a front-end to sales. We generated leads with marketing programs, and used inside sales staff to qualify leads and set meetings for outside sales. Hence, a new direct salesperson coming into the company would be going on meetings the first week, rather than trying to jump-start a stone cold territory. Our ramp times were significantly faster than what I have observed in other companies where salespeople are handed a "bag" and told to go out and find business. Work is work, but marketing and inside sales are much more cost-effective than having super-expensive direct sales staff do cold prospecting work (which they are not even very good at!).

Chapter 6
Figuring out the channel

Coming from enterprise software where selling is mostly direct, we were curious what resellers really did for a living, especially in the US. Internationally, resellers acted more as full franchise holders of our business in their local markets; the domestic resellers were getting paid on deals, but what precisely was their value added in the process?

Startups often think the recipe is to sign up some resellers and wait for phone calls announcing deals in the works—wrong. Resellers don't work for you; they have their own constituencies. Resellers start getting interested when their bread-and-butter customers begin asking about your product, and even then they first go back to their mainline suppliers to see if they have something similar. Years of profitable relationships will not be overturned because you have a cool new contraption.

Data Domain got traction in the channel in a few ways. First, we had our own direct sales function. It is hard to overstate the importance of having your own muscle on the street. You won't take us in? Fine—we will go on our own, and bring in *your* competition. Second, we will take you to the mat while we're there, meaning we will flatly sell *your* customer *our* product. Now, the reseller begins to wonder (if not panic) which side they should be on. We had resellers leave and re-join us more than once: each time, a big supplier forced them to drop us, and then suffered beatings by us in front of the customer. They bet on the wrong horse, and it drove them crazy. Your power is in your own sales function and product—keep that in mind.

Another tactic that worked was an all-channel policy. Big suppliers always had a stratified channel program in which major enterprise accounts were taken direct, and mid-market customers were left to the channel. Data Domain put all its business through the channel: when the mainline suppliers shut them out of their big enterprise accounts, we took them in. In addition, in every deal we worked on our own, we introduced a reseller to the deal to get them a little bit "pregnant" with Data Domain. It is hard to say no to deals being thrown in your lap—of course, we expected the favor to be returned.

Did this all-channel policy affect our margin profile? Not as much as you might think. Enterprise customers fully realize there is more discount to be had when there is no man in the middle. We demonstrated that direct and indirect deals in the aggregate did not differ materially in profitability.

That is how we busted through these entrenched relationships: in the end, it is a matter of them not being able to get around you. Success doesn't come because they think you have a cool product—it is a power game, so play it that way. Your power is your ability to get directly to the end customer.

The channel is a powerful, entrenched fixture in the industry, and one that demands respect. If you don't bring the channel in, they will bring in your competition. Customers use resellers as a check on suppliers, knowing that resellers jeopardize their customer relationship if they bring in an unvetted dud. Some resellers—the best ones—have deep technical staffs to support customers, and are a value-add in the sales process.

I regarded some of the domestic channel more as a lead-generation activity than a sales channel, but this perspective was not always shared inside our company. We insisted on going in with the reseller to qualify the opportunity. We also wanted to drive and sell the deal ourselves—without your presence, the reseller may just decide to switch horses and bring in a competitor.

Your channel goal is to assure that resellers register opportunities with you; in turn, you protect their registrations from other resellers. We administered a large margin differential between registered and unregistered deals. It was hard but not impossible to crash somebody else's deal on price with the same Data Domain product. We carefully kept track of quarterly lead registration trends as our leading indicator for channel contribution.

The channel must be actively managed to your advantage. It will not be neutral to your business—it is either helping or hurting. The channel has its own interests and constituents, and you can feed, educate, and cater to them, or somebody else will.

Chapter 7
Know when to hold, know when to fold

Running a startup sometimes feels like a game of cards in which you have no control over the hand you are dealt: basically, the company as you found it. All you can do is play the cards you hold the best way you know how. A big part of playing the game is how—and how fast—you invest the available resources of the company.

When you are not yet generating revenue, conservation of resources is the dominant theme. I am puzzled by ventures that try to generate "buzz," as if that is something you can take to the bank. Too much buzz too early, and you may get taken out prematurely, unable to fully realize the potential of the business. The buzz thing seems like a plea for reassurance that one indeed has a worthy venture, something that caters to one's insecurities rather than a good use of marketing resources.

Yet, there comes a time when the venture must pivot from conserving resources to applying them rapidly, as fast as you know how to do effectively—when that cross-over time comes is not always obvious. The irony is that most ventures seem to spend too much early on, and not enough later on when they could grow faster and pay for it. The question becomes "can you grow faster?" And, if not, why not? That should be a good board meeting discussion.

The turning point comes when your sales activity is solidly paying for itself, and is clearly becoming more profitable with increasing volume. Now you have a virtual money machine and you want to start opening the floodgates. Growing rapidly is something you also have to plan for; you cannot just start piling on bodies with a pulse, blowing money on marketing. The business will start thrashing. Hiring additional salespeople can be nerve-wracking because if they don't get traction quickly, you have to shift gears. Sales people get "pruned" much more quickly in an early-stage venture: you cannot afford to wait an entire growing season to decide if a new branch is going to bear fruit.

Successful ventures grow on an S-curve: the early years are quite slow and flat, then the inflection comes—hopefully—and the business has the potential to go near vertical. Two key questions are (a) do you know when that is, and (b) are you prepared at that point to fully invest for growth? Preparing an organization for growth before it actually happens takes poise, like building Noah's Ark when no meaningful amounts of rain had been recorded for years.

To use another image, a venture-backed startup is like a space shuttle: it gets launched with booster rockets (venture capital) and has to last long enough to break the pull of gravity (break-even). Once you've achieved escape velocity, you jettison the rockets and fly under your own power. If you run out of booster fuel prematurely, the venture will drop back down to earth—a mental model on how to think about cash.

In the company's cash-negative years, you manage from one fund-raising event to another and need to set explicit milestones to enable the company to raise money at fair valuations. The question becomes: what proof points do we need to have in terms of product, customers, business model, and so on to be able to bring on a new lead investor in a strong up-round? Having replenished the rockets, sights are set and a realistic course is charted to achieve the next set of milestones. Startups often enter into fundraising ill prepared, not having accomplished enough to attract top quality investors, or having to settle for a lesser valuation than may seem warranted.

When I joined Data Domain, I almost immediately had to start raising the B-series round of funding, as A-series money was on the verge of running out (a matter of months). I quickly realized we did not have enough data points to support the effort. (If you are groveling in front of VCs, you're probably not ready.) We pulled back, doubled down on closing our early betas into paying, happy customers, and went back out three months later, backed by fresh, walking-talking, flesh-and-blood data points. The B-round got done at a decent valuation, the fuel tanks were replenished, and we fine-tuned a trajectory to propel us onward for the next 18 months.

Chapter 8
In transition

A time came in our journey when the company was hitting a ceiling on scale—the organization had grown unwieldy. Something was wrong: we had more dysfunction and did not know why. Looking back, we had entered the transition from infancy to early adolescence. We were like 5-year-olds playing soccer, a mob of kids following the ball all over the field with nobody playing position. We had outgrown the early stage when everything is fluid and instantaneous and the team practically functions as a single organism.

We were stingy on hiring managers quickly enough. We hired mostly people who could be individual contributors, e.g., sell stuff, build stuff, and support stuff—everybody was hands-on, from the CEO on down. Hardly anybody had "just" a management job. We needed to begin building out a management tier to multiply the organization's ability to grow itself—then we realized we didn't necessarily have all the right people for this part of the journey, either.

The first time we brought in engineering managers below the VP of Engineering, many engineers said almost in unison, "We don't need no stinking managers! We can manage ourselves, like we have been." It was an adjustment, all right. Dan McGee, Data Domain's head of engineering, had his hands full taking over this engineering team, which he ended up scaling more than ten-fold over the next four years. On the sales side, we had hired guys with quota who sold every day, all day; now we needed sales managers whose role was to recruit and manage performance and activity. Could we afford the "overhead"?

The new people were like WWII allied replenishment troops who had not experienced the jump into Normandy—they were not immediately viewed with the same combat respect as the men and women of the first hour. That sentiment didn't last long, however, as new challenges and struggles brought us together quickly.

Once the management tiers took shape, the organization leapt forward—we were becoming professional. We were still a lightweight management organization, but we gained much-needed process, structure, protocol, and controls—the stuff you need to be able to function with a rapidly growing group of people. You simply cannot ingest lots of people if there is no defined model underpinning how they fit into the organization.

We had cracked some of the code, and it became continuous, rapid cell division—as long as the math worked, we kept multiplying. The math tests related to what operating expense categories had to be at target levels of revenues. In sales, it was a productivity calculation: we needed to stay ahead of the ratio of sales-expense dollars as a percent of revenues. A motivated, well-compensated sales team can often close business, but if their commission incentives and pricing flexibility are allowed to surrender too much margin, the economics won't work. Sales has to pay for itself and for the cost of goods, with some margin left over to pay other expenses of the business. Low-margin businesses have this problem and don't scale well; they don't get much more profitable as they grow larger.

Data Domain was in hyper growth: our math was designed to fuel the rocket, which is very different from a low growth, steady-state business. We judged the business more on a cash basis rather than formal profit and loss statements—cash over costs, bookings over revenue.

Accounting is the bastardization of economics. It can be puzzling to see early stage ventures focusing on P&L profitability, as that mentality can choke off growth in a hurry. You should not care much about profits early on. Instead, you care about maximizing growth while maintaining sufficient cash balances to sustain it.

Our first three years of sales were wildly unprofitable because, from an accounting perspective, we had not achieved so-called VSOE. This forced us to recognize all revenue ratably over the contract period, including system sales, not just our multi-year support contracts with customers. Never mind, though: we collected cash right away, often also for the entire support term. This all started to matter by the time of our IPO, but in the early stages these were abstract concepts. I have seen startups managing for profitability prematurely—a huge mistake. They simply do not appreciate the dynamics of an early stage, high growth operation versus a large, steady-state company. Big company thinking: check it at the door.

Data Domain had gained a fresh appreciation of what value management really added. In big companies it is rarely questioned, accepted as part of the overhead; in a startup, you justify management in the most elementary terms.

In addition to not ushering in management tiers fast enough, I made other mistakes. I was stingy on hiring administrative staff: we ran the company up to 40-50 million dollars in annual sales with two people in finance. When we hired our first CFO, Mike Scarpelli, and then Ron Codd as audit committee chairman on the board, they rightly questioned my sanity. Nobody got hurt, luckily—Mike addressed it in record time. Don't do as I did!

You may wonder how a guy like me, who has spent most of his life in larger companies, didn't see this coming— fair question. Running a startup reduces you to your most elementary instincts, and survival is on your mind most of the time. I became very calculating about what resources were needed to stay alive, conserving most everything else. We hated raising capital—it was distracting to the business and diluted equity. As time went on, we eased up on this wild animal mentality but we never totally lost it. When EMC acquired us, they were surprised—if not slightly puzzled—to see how tight, disciplined, and cost-conscious Data Domain was. They were perhaps expecting the stereotypical, free-spending West Coast operation without adult supervision. What they got was a lean, mean, fighting machine.

In general, when growing an organization, look hard at balancing resources and look at every category of spending and hiring. If you under-resource one area, you may hamstring the entire organization—you can become unhinged. We had that in the operations and manufacturing function: being a software guy, I had insufficient appreciation for the level of resources required here, and the leadership was hesitant in making the case. It was my mistake, not trusting the organization enough, until we got a grizzled manufacturing veteran, Nick Bacica, to head up Data Domain Operations. Nick told me in no uncertain terms what I had to do; I listened and just gave him what he requested. We'd had close calls already.

What I learned here is that when you do not trust the advice you are getting, it is time to shift gears—even if there are no other glaring issues at hand. It is key to have strong executives who know what level of resources they need and when, and who will make that case with unyielding conviction. I would push back, but primarily to test the resolve behind the numbers. Trust your team— nothing else scales.

Chapter 9
Hire athletes, not resumes

Hiring can be very challenging for early stage ventures because they are unproven and high risk. New hires often have to take pay cuts. Looking for the perfect resume is a bit like a man looking for the perfect woman—when he finds her, it turns out she is looking for the perfect man, and he ain't it! Moral of the story: it is hard to land a candidate who meets your resume criteria, as you are not that good a catch yet yourself.

After suffering through a few instances of this mismatch at Data Domain, we adjusted our search algorithm and began looking for candidates who did not have the resume yet but did have the potential and desire for a career break to get to the next level. We called them "athletes": candidates with the right aptitude and behavior profile but without the prerequisite experience.

Put differently, we started looking for people who we thought had their best work still in front of them, rather than behind them. How did we know? You can't just rely on resume or references—you are making a bet that they can become what you need them to be. We looked for energy, pedigree, passion, ambition, intelligence, intensity, and desire for the job. We staffed many (if not most) of our executive and key managerial roles that way.

Our approach worked so well that we started to prefer this style of hiring, even later on when we could attract "resumes." In fact, it drove a vital ingredient of the Data Domain culture: everybody had something to prove.

The thinking to "hire athletes, not resumes" has grown more accepted in recent years, and startups have adjusted to this style of hiring. But there was a time when it was hard to get past the "resume mentality," e.g., just looking for all the boxes to be checked. We stumbled upon our way of thinking by sheer necessity, yet it grew into a key component of the Data Domain success formula.

Chapter 10
Fail fast

I am not sure who first coined the saying "fail fast," but the idea is that once it becomes apparent you have made a mistake, own up to it and begin deliberating alternative action. In organizations, people often become hardened defenders of their decisions because they fear it will reflect poorly on them if they admit a mistake; however, all this does is slow down the necessary adjustment. Big companies are sometimes able to survive this type of dysfunction, but startups are so fragile—they threaten their existence by staying on the wrong path too long. An organization can be quite effective just in being a rapid course-corrector.

How do you get your organization to behave with a fail-fast mentality? First, start at the top. Lead by example: quickly and publicly acknowledge your mistakes, and move on. Act matter of fact-ly. I've had to clean up my own messes for everybody to see. Talk about it publicly, what you were thinking at the time, what was learned from it; this signals to the organization that it is okay to make mistakes and openly own them.

Second, do not allow a culture that penalizes mistakes and keeps score. Everybody who makes decisions is going to make mistakes—it is how swiftly we deal with a mistake that matters. You don't have to be perfect, but we do require you to be intellectually honest about how your decisions pan out.

Because the Data Domain culture was so direct and upfront, it would have been hard to hide mistakes anyhow. If you didn't come to the right conclusion yourself, the rest of us would point it out for you quickly enough. Once established by example, it is not hard for people to be this way. Speed is the essence of a startup: we have to be able to take mistakes in stride, and self-correct in the normal course of business.

Chapter 11
Big banks, a target vertical?

Big financials buying your product is often seen as the ultimate validation; boards sometimes like to see some early success there, and drive management teams to set up shop in the major financial centers. Data Domain's experience was dismal in the beginning. We didn't have the scale, maturity, and feature set to really address these ultra-demanding accounts.

Moreover, financial institutions are notoriously conservative, preferring their suppliers to be the pillars of the industry, not some fledgling startup. They see themselves as aggressive adopters of technology, but that pertains only to certain applications. In datacenter infrastructure, they seem slower to move than the marketplace at large. Also, because of the big banks' size and scale, sales processes are lengthy, consuming, and intensely political—not what startups are geared for.

We would have starved to death maintaining focus on this vertical. As a startup, you need to be opportunist: you sell where you can. Smart salespeople instinctively gravitate to the shortest distance between them and a sale. It is hard enough as it is.

The key is to discover where you can get traction, and then step it up—develop best practices and share them instantly. Data Domain's sales organization sometimes acted like a single organism: it was constantly communicating, assessing, and synthesizing what it needed to do to sell. Everybody helped everybody else in real time. Newly hired salespeople were stunned that they could pose a question online, and responses started piling up within minutes.

Where you hit the proverbial brick wall, back away and re-allocate to other segments. In Data Domain's case, we were well equipped for the mid-market and the channel. That's where we got traction while flying under the radar for a long time, building our install base, maturing our products, and delighting customers. From the mid-market we gradually moved up to larger accounts as our products scaled and matured; we gradually sneaked up on the "big boys."

Chapter 12
In the thick of things

The CEO is the "Chief Combatant," warrior number one. Instilling a fighting spirit into your company is key to winning in the market place. CEOs can't manage from behind the desk—you need to be the first guy or gal over the barricades, gloves off. You need to know from experience what it's like getting your nose bloodied; otherwise, your troops can't relate to you and you can't relate to them.

I put myself in contentious sales situations. Not just to hone our game, but show the organization we had no fear—that we'd take on anybody, no matter how few letters there were in the company name. I staked out the Greater Boston Area and made more sales calls in the Northeast than anywhere else. Why? It was the home of our principal competitor at the time, EMC. We wanted to show our people we could beat them in their own backyard.

With my history as a product manager, this was familiar territory. I spent most of my working life getting called into accounts when the deal was on the line and the local salesperson needed a small miracle. If you come from the sales side, this should be innate to you as well. But if you don't naturally swarm to the action, you need to learn that attitude.

Aside from the leadership value, being at the transfer point from technology to sales is critical to understanding your business and how it evolves. Few things were more inspiring and motivating than a few days on the road seeing 5-6 accounts a day. I'd get back to the ranch, anxious to share the experience and feedback with the team. If you don't do enough of this, you won't be very good at it, and you will gradually become more removed from everything. You are much closer to your own troops being in the thick of things.

I liken business to a combination of contact sport and warfare; people don't get killed in the game, but companies do. We were gunning for the competition. Employees needed to feel the cold winds of competitive threat on a daily basis. Their mental attitude to the job needed to be honed by both the threat and the opportunity. At Data Domain, we vilified and demonized the competition with our employees. Our head of sales, David Schneider, always sent out colorful notes on big wins with all the salient, polemic details. Who did we beat, and how did we beat them? Our employees fed on that information, hungry for news from the battlefields of technology.

Chapter 13
Show some humanity!

Among many hats, the CEO serves as the leader of the band, and he or she must firmly step into that role; everybody in the company wants to know you and get a sense of your personality, who you really are. Many executives get in front of an audience and they become stiff, scripted, rehearsed, politically-correct, and put up a wall so it is hard for the audience to "know" them. It is an understandable response and few of us are naturals at this, but that is not how you want to be with your people.

People can instantly finger a phony. Let them know who you really are, warts and all—show your humanity, your passions, your likes and dislikes. What do you feel strongly about? Can they still remember what you said a week later? Are you leaving a room with more energy than when you entered it? Not sure? Then you didn't.

For most of us, it is work to become an authentic leader. By *authentic* I mean being who you really are versus acting out some burnished version of you. People respond to key attributes that you want to highlight: your determination, passion, energy, intensity, and no-holds-barred desire to succeed no matter what. Chances are you have those in spades or you wouldn't be where you are.

Whatever you are passionate about, make sure it is out there for all to see.

In my own time, I competed in triathlons, a personal passion at the time. In 2009 we participated in the Escape from Alcatraz triathlon with five Data Domain relay teams. The whole company got involved—after all, we were competing against other Bay Area tech companies!

In addition, I often said controversial (sometimes outrageous) things that were published in the press—not just to be quotable, but for our own troops to read. Show off some of the color and texture in your personality.

Press and analysts often needled me with the comment that IBM and Symantec with their armies of engineers could build this technology in six months and put us out of business. I responded that while "you can throw a thousand women at the task of making a baby, it is still going to take nine months!" I shocked some folks with the metaphor, but they sure remembered. How else to make the point that technology has a gestation period regardless of resources? Worse, software development actually suffers from diseconomies of scale: the more engineers, the slower it goes.

In conclusion, put yourself out there! As is clear from popular media, people have a fascination with public personas. Well, guess what? You are one inside your own company.

Chapter 14
It is not about you

Let's face it, CEOs have sizable egos. You need one to even want to be at the top, but you need to put that irrepressible ego in the service of the company. How many companies do you know where the CEO suffers from some form of megalomania, perpetually buzzed with the powers vested in him/her? Did it feel like the company was there for further aggrandizement of the CEO? Some companies can endure this type of regime, but for others, it sucks the life out of them. Remember that CEOs of venture-backed startups do not own the company—the investors do.

Pat Lencioni's book, *The Five Dysfunctions of a Team*, nails this topic under the header "absence of trust." One year at a Data Domain management off-site, we all read the book in preparation, then discussed openly how much we suffered from these dysfunctions as a team—they sneak up on you, and you may learn things that are disconcerting. It's like holding a mirror in front of you: is that what I look like?

I have known CEOs who were blissfully unaware of how their own egos were front and center in every dealing, but for everybody else it was plain to see. For things to work, you need a strong, grounded team around you that is not afraid to tell you—to your face—what they really think. If you don't have that, or are not sure, the emperor is probably already running around naked.

Good CEOs seem to have a measure of introspection, able to see themselves largely the way other people see them; this is essential to gain authenticity as a leader. That said, we all have blind spots, some more than others. When the company does well, CEOs get most of the credit and heads swell, compounding the problem. It's hard work keeping this in check and deflecting the credit back to the organization. It is not I but *you* who collectively made this happen! Never miss an opportunity to shower your organization with praise—they deserve it.

In my own experience, as a leader I did not really strive for personal recognition from the company journey. My intensity, focus, and energy came from an overwhelming fear of failure. I could not stand the thought of failing, and I could not face our organization in defeat—that insecurity was the rocket fuel in my personal tank. We all have our demons; the challenge is to channel them in a constructive way. Let it help the cause, not hurt it.

One symptom of a leader too focused on him/herself is the tendency to always speak in the first person. "I, my, mine," instead of "we, ours, us." Even the President of the United States always talks about "my administration," but it is not his—it is the people's. CEOs who talk about "my guys," "my CFO," or "my company" subliminally send the wrong message. It takes a little awareness to turn this around by always talking about the company plural and avoiding the urge to personalize. It is not about you; indeed, you can't afford for it to be.

Chapter 15
Selling abroad early

The prevailing wisdom in the venture world was to prove the recipe at home before going abroad, but Data Domain didn't entirely comply with this notion. First, as a European I saw nothing alien about starting a sales activity over there. Second, we started getting inquiries and interest from Europe and Japan. Why blow them off? We decided to see what happened first. As said before, be an opportunist—when opportunity comes from unexpected places, why not go with it? See where it leads.

Our board wasn't thrilled with our early foreign explorations, seeing it as a lack of focus. We wanted to appoint an executive-level role over there, and they didn't support that. We ended up getting somebody willing to join us in a non-executive capacity; he did very well in that role, and eventually was elevated anyway.

Our business overseas wasn't huge, but we started to figure out the channel game over there, the differences between national markets, and we started occupying strategic positions with key partners and customers long before our competition even got wind of it. It takes a long time to develop a sales infrastructure anywhere, so you might as well get started. Once partners invest in your business, they will not easily switch horses as long as they are successful.

In Data Domain's case, we had huge early take-up in Scandinavia and Sweden in particular, totally disproportionate to the size of the market there. Why? We had a reseller named ProAct in Stockholm take a strong interest very early on. The additional sales were welcome, but ProAct was a great development partner for us as well, providing very pointed feedback to our product teams that paid dividends for us in all future sales.

It is more common now to see ventures seek overseas opportunity early—the world has become quite small. Our global language, transportation, and communication infrastructure enables this. Moral of the story: don't let dated bias hold you back from sniffing out overseas opportunities.

Chapter 16
The board doesn't run the company

The board doesn't run the company—you do. The board oversees the company from a governance standpoint, but its fundamental role and power is to hire and fire the CEO; it delegates its power to the CEO on a day-to-day basis. However, the protocol between CEO and startup board seems to be poorly defined and subject to interpretation. Some boards are more removed from operations, whereas others can barely restrain themselves from grabbing the steering wheel.

A lot of this has to do with trust, or lack thereof: as a rule, boards start to assert themselves more the less they trust the CEO. CEOs often pander to boards and cannot resist a tendency to be promotional at board meetings. You want a CEO who can present a thoughtful analysis with all the pros and cons, not a promotional pitch on how great things are. You want people who have an accurate grasp of the gap that exists between where things stand and what is aimed for. CEOs must lead. Boards step in the moment they perceive a leadership vacuum.

When I first became CEO of Data Domain, board member Scott Sandell of NEA said, "I just want transparency and intellectual honesty." It gave me a context on how to deal with our board. In the spirit of Clint Eastwood, our board-meeting theme was "the good, the bad, and the ugly." Board meetings were a time where I shared some of the hell between my ears with everybody else. They always asked, "what is keeping you up at night?" and sometimes got more than they bargained for. We had a strong board; they handled it well.

I carried this too far at times, and when the company became a rocket ship some of our board members could not understand why I wasn't in a better frame of mind. I was making them paranoid! The paranoia never leaves you—there rarely was a time we felt comfortable congratulating one another. At the end of a strong quarter, we were already deep into planning the next one. We walked around with a combat mentality, guns and machetes drawn.

A new board and CEO would benefit from discussing the protocol they want: where, how, and when does the board get involved with operations? Without explicit clarity, people will make it up—power fills a vacuum. In our case, trust grew because we earned it over time, and the board delegated more and more. At Data Domain, executive appointments or changes in executive compensation always required board review. Why? I didn't want to make these decisions without oversight. All other decisions were made with at least one other layer of management overseeing, but in the case of CEO decisions, there isn't another layer of management. This policy prepared us well for becoming a public company where this is de rigueur.

Board members can become prescriptive in their dealings with the CEO and the other executives. In Silicon Valley board meetings, you are inevitably lectured on the successes of companies that came before you, as if that were the only credible source of guidance and wisdom. You guys should be more like company A, they did this, or company B, they did that, etc. We rolled our eyes. Nowadays I feel badly for companies that are lectured on the success of Data Domain! I don't believe in running the same playbook twice. We didn't have a playbook—it came about as we went along.

The risk is that the team starts to take orders from the board. Silicon Valley boards tend to be made up of accomplished individuals with no shortage of opinions, and they can quickly lapse into a "been-there, done-that" command mode. But all the board can do is give you ways to think about issues and problems—you and your team decide if and how it applies. You live with the decisions you make, so the decisions have to be yours. There is a fuzzy line here where the board may try to influence decisions that are really in your purview. Don't be a pleaser, and don't be an appeaser. Do what you think is right. Do anything less, and you only have yourself to blame.

The company is a ship that comes into port periodically to report on business. The board members come aboard for the meeting but trundle safely ashore afterward, while ship, captain, and crew go back out to sea, facing whatever is out there. We are the ones lashed to the mast; we will go down with the ship. The board holds interest in a whole fleet of ships, but we, the employees, just have the one we're on—it is profoundly not the same.

Aneel Bhusri of Greylock became our board chairman and lead director, bringing extensive operational background from his years at Peoplesoft. Over time, Aneel evolved his role to making sure the board functioned properly and didn't impede the company's growth. It was extremely valuable for me as CEO to have a chairman like Aneel. I could have been bogged down in a lot of board gyrations, but thanks to him I rarely was. He was a trusted counselor but also a close comrade who was comfortable being shoulder-to-shoulder with us in our foxhole, especially during the IPO process and when the bidding war for the company ensued.

Scott Sandell of NEA had a different style—he was the quintessential investor. With a huge board load, he was the least inclined to cross the invisible line between governance and operations. But while he would rarely impose himself on the company, he'd be available instantly to you if you called on him. His rich and deep investing experience left him with an unusual ability to pattern match our operations against those that went before. He had this style about him leaving no doubt that while he would share his point of view, he was not making recommendations or prescriptions: you, the CEO, were the judge. It actually made it easier to seek him out, as he didn't demand you follow his point of view. He impressed on me that the role of the board was to hire and fire the CEO, and that he would not hesitate to pull either trigger!

Ron Bernal, at the time from Sutter Hill Ventures, was much more of an operator than an investor in the early days. As the company grew, he was a godsend as he helped us make contacts and identify candidates for roles in places where our own Rolodex was sparse. He had a rich history of working inside Cisco and SGI that yielded many valuable contacts and insights along the way. Ron's mentality was always "how can I help?" When boards aren't healthy, the CEO can feel caught in the crossfire of carping, coercing, and hidden agendas; Data Domain never struggled with this, and Ron's pure servant mode was a big part of the reason.

One thing to keep in mind is that a company can outgrow its board's range of experience. None of our board members had recent experience, if any at all, with the type of hyper growth we experienced. When was the last time one had gone through an IPO? Bidding war? It was new to them, too.

I remember one year hearing NFL great John Madden on local radio with the brand new coach of the Stanford Cardinals football team, Jim Harbaugh. Harbaugh asked if Madden had any words of wisdom for him as he started a new coaching job. Madden said that he would encounter many well-intentioned people with opinions on how to run the football team, who to draft, what plays to run;

they could be alumni, benefactors, university brass, etc. Madden told Harbaugh to keep his own counsel and make his own decisions because "when you win, they can't hurt you, and when you lose they can't help you." Jim Harbaugh of the Stanford Cardinals seems to have taken that advice to heart judging from results!

I found this advice priceless. You might as well spend all your time on winning—nothing else matters. Of course, a good board wants you to do exactly that. It obviously doesn't mean you should blindly bat away all opinions coming at you, but just try them on for size and merit, and go from there. Keeping good council is strength; caving in on perceived pressure is weakness.

Chapter 17
Going public

Data Domain went public on Nasdaq in June of 2007, about 5.5 years after its inception and four years after I joined. We had already been operating cash-positive for some time—we did not really need to raise capital for operations. So, why did we go?

First, when you compete with giants, you always face the customer's insecurity of doing business with a smaller vendor, a private company whose balance sheet and P&L are not out in the open. The IPO became a giant marketing debut for the company. It was a brand thing: we were serving notice to customers, competitors, and investors alike that we were coming out, raising a war chest, and not going anywhere. Becoming a public company helped level the playing field. David was girding to take on an array of serious Goliaths, but there was still a long way to go.

Second, we were a venture-backed startup, with the majority of the company's stock held by three venture firms. Venture investors get in to get out, and they can only get out through a company sale or through the capital markets. We needed a liquid market for investors to trade in and out of our equity. Aside from our venture shareholders, the common stock was in the hands of employees—they obviously also deserve an opportunity to monetize some of their holdings after years of slaving away, often at below-market pay.

Third, operating as a public company imposes a new level of operating discipline. There is a lot of noise about how confining the capital markets can be to a company, and there is truth to that. You are under a microscope, operating in the open for everybody to see; the quarterly earnings circus can dampen a long-term strategy. On the other hand, execution must improve when publicly traded—it will force the company to deal with many issues that previously didn't seem as important or urgent. Your systems and processes must be bulletproof. Mistakes like earnings restatements cost public companies dearly, whereas in the private realm it would be a minor matter.

Data Domain transitioned its board of directors in preparation for the IPO. Kai Li, as the lead founder, and the three venture board members stayed on, but we added directors who could credibly staff board committees such as comp and audit. We were pleased to have Ron Codd, former long-time CFO of Peoplesoft join us on audit, and Jeff Miller, the former CEO of Documentum head our compensation committee. Reed Hundt, former Chairman of the FCC under President Clinton and an Intel board member rounded out the seasoned new board additions.

Investors scrutinize board credentials to make sure there are experienced adults overseeing the new high-fliers. Keeping in mind that the IPO is largely a marketing event, one goal is to add some brand to your board. It is also a prime opportunity to round out your board: recruit individuals who bring the right industry experience and who are ready to challenge your thinking. Our three additions would do this well for us.

A lot of CEOs who have crossed through the looking glass from private to public will tell you that the constraints, regulatory overhead, and quarterly obsession will forever handcuff you—this is an exaggeration. As a public company, you still have room to move in terms of how you wish to operate the company, but you better learn to explain those moves in terms the markets can readily understand. Don't fall into the trap of letting sell-side analysts dictate your strategy. They will be the first to say, "don't listen to us," but like Greek sailors lured by the mythical sirens, lots of companies become slaves to Wall Street expectations because they think it will lead to short-term stock price appreciation. Take a deep breath and steel your resolve before you go public. You are going to need it.

As to timing, you go out when you can. The IPO window needs to be open, meaning that institutional investors are in a mood to look at new issues. As near as I can tell, the IPO window opens and shuts without warning. It takes at least six months from the time you decide to go, to actually being out, and three of those months just to get on file with the SEC. A lot can happen in that period: markets cool, news happens, opinions and expectations change. So, you see many IPO filings pulled while queuing on the runway. Your company needs to be far enough along where you can achieve a market cap that puts the company in a solid trading zone. Investors want to be able to take positions large enough to be worth their while, yet small enough they can easily trade in/out of their position. Lacking market cap and liquidity (regardless of the core strength of your business) will cause problems.

So, to review: If you lack enough revenue, growth, and profitability, you don't want to be public. Likewise, if your quarterly results are unpredictable, you don't want to be public. Remember, you will need to guide the market for the quarter and the year as a public company, so your operating discipline better be such that you can hit your guidance. Put the training wheels on early—start guiding your board while still private, and make sure it works.

As an economic mechanism, the "Initial Public Offering" process is a strange combination of raw market forces, extreme regulation, institutional signaling, and celebrated ritual. Pre-IPO companies have more options these days, with secondary exchanges enabling employees and investors to liquidate some of their holdings, staving off some of the pressure to go public. Some pundits forecast the demise of the IPO market in the face of these new vehicles to gain liquidity and currency. But as much as the traditional IPO is in transition, no clear replacement has yet emerged.

Data Domain was taken out by Goldman Sachs and Morgan Stanley as joint book runners. Because your IPO is likely your company's biggest marketing debut ever, we preferred to go out with big-name Wall Street firms—it signals high confidence and demand for your IPO. If you go out with a second- or third-tier bank, investors may wonder why. IPOs are hard, so you want every advantage you can get. Investors took note of our IPO because we had two Wall Street titans who rarely ever appear together on the cover of an offering. They are like the Israelis and the Palestinians: they will only tolerate working together if they simply cannot afford to be left out. And the market appreciates that.

The IPO roadshow was exactly two weeks, in which we pitched approximately 100 investors all over the US and Europe. About 95 came "into the book," meaning they bought into the offering. An IPO roadshow is like speed selling—you have 10 meetings a day, and you need to close each in about 30-40 minutes, or less. The CEO does 90% of the talking. It has been said that the CFO has the hardest job as he or she has to listen to the CEO's roadshow pitch a hundred times in two weeks!

At the end of the roadshow, your bankers price the stock in consultation with you. It is a contentious process—you want higher, they want lower. Everybody is posturing and positioning. In our case, we could not get them to move one quarter above $15 bucks, and then the stock traded up to $20 the first day. It seems everybody has the same experience: the IPO buyers get rewarded with a nice initial run-up pretty much built in to the IPO price. Momentum matters. You want your IPO to trade up some, but not too much or you are leaving money on the table!

Chapter 18
Getting acquired

Data Domain was acquired in a high profile bidding war in the summer of 2009, about two years after going public. It must have been a slow news period as we were on CNBC every day, providing entertainment to the industry. We had our 15 minutes of fame, all right. We signed a definitive agreement to be acquired by NetApp in May for $25 a share, and ten days later EMC came over the transom with a tender offer of $30 a share directly to our shareholders. NetApp matched the offer, and a month-long DOJ investigation ensued under the Hart-Scott-Rodino Act.

Every deal of some size has to be reviewed by either the FTC or DOJ for antitrust considerations, but in this case NetApp campaigned against EMC on antitrust grounds because they would surely be outgunned by EMC on price. Hence, the government had to go through even more motions than usual. We sat on pins and needles responding to requests for information from the government for the next 3-4 weeks. Finally, both bidders were waved on by the government. Just before the July 4th recess, EMC raised its bid to $33.50, and NetApp conceded.

EMC's offer was all cash and NetApp was part cash, part stock; cash offers have so called "certainty of value" that is important to shareholders. NetApp pointed out in hindsight that our shareholders would have been better off with their offer because NetApp's stock rallied so much in the aftermath, but that was impossible to know at the time. Had it gone the other way, Data Domain's turning down an all-cash superior offer would have triggered a litany of litigation for our board. Those investors bullish on the NetApp offer could have simply taken the superior EMC offer and re-invested the proceeds in NetApp stock.

Over the years, I had met Dan Warmenhoven, the CEO of NetApp, and maintained a cordial rapport with him in spite of the fact that we were competitors. It certainly raised our comfort level being acquired by NetApp—a good cultural fit, we all thought. EMC, on the other hand, was our archenemy. I had never met Joe Tucci, the CEO of EMC, or even spoken to him prior to the definitive agreement being signed with EMC. You can imagine we had some trepidation. EMC, the evil empire!

So, why did we sell? This was the hardest decision our board had ever faced. I initiated the process after a meeting I had at a Los Gatos diner with Tom Georgens, then COO of NetApp, and today the company's CEO. The timing was March 2009. It was the roughest quarter yet for Data Domain, and anybody else in our sector. We had started to slow down sequentially even though our year-on-year growth was still off the chart. We were competing in the big leagues, but we still had a relatively narrow product offering that was vulnerable to portfolio selling by competition.

It was the old squeeze play. A more precise term for this is "predatory pricing"—basically, our competition charged minimal dollars for our component as part of a much larger transaction. We had trouble qualifying for RFPs because our product offering was not broad enough. We couldn't partner, either, because potential partners all wanted us dead! At the same time, companies like Oracle, HP, IBM, and Cisco had started to broaden their ability to act as one-stop shops for the entire data center. Maintaining our growth was key, and we concluded that we needed to become part of a broader product and services portfolio to win in the biggest accounts and continue to spread the gospel of deduplication. There were plenty of rumors then of NetApp being acquired as well. The winds of change were blowing.

EMC dramatically accelerated the Data Domain business. We grew in excess of 100% year-on-year in each of the next five quarters—huge growth for a business as large as ours. There is no doubt that EMC put rocket fuel in our tank with their global sales and distribution channels. As we had hoped, the acquisition had boosted our trajectory yet again.

Could we have achieved loftier heights on our own? It is impossible to know. EMC did extremely well with the acquisition, Data Domain shareholders did spectacularly well—everybody won. Even NetApp, which had hoped to acquire Data Domain, fared just fine in the aftermath.

Chapter 19
Post-acquisition

We completed the acquisition of Data Domain by EMC, shares got tendered, and that was that. The Monday after the definitive agreement was signed with EMC, 15 or so EMC executives showed up on our doorstep in Santa Clara at 9:00 am. We sat in our boardroom and discussed how to go forward.

I met Joe Tucci later that day, and had dinner with him that evening; he proved to be a real gentleman and a high integrity guy. He protected Data Domain against the EMC bureaucracy, which in hindsight was quite necessary. We knew he had done it before for VMware, and we benefitted from the same firewall approach—no doubt he will do this again for Isilon, EMC's latest announced multi-billion-dollar acquisition.

Joe asked us to use Data Domain as a platform for a new EMC division that would include all of EMC data protection product lines. We would double in size overnight. I wasn't that keen on running anything other than Data Domain, but realized that we would confuse the customer base and our own people if we did not take control of all these products that had competed so fiercely in the marketplace. And so we did. The new division was called EMC BRS for Backup Recovery

Systems. We became the fastest growing EMC division in the next 18 months, posting even bigger year-on-year growth numbers than the golden child, VMWare. While VMWare was EMC's best acquisition hands down, when asked, EMC will tell you that Data Domain is running a solid second.

You may wonder why I stuck around—I didn't need to. I had no contractual or financial requirements, so I could have walked on day one. Except, I wasn't ready to leave. Our culture was so invested in the success of the business, how could I just walk away? I did not want to incite attrition or instability in the organization by virtue of my abrupt absence. I also felt I could protect the business against incursions from the EMC bureaucracy. Many acquisitions fizzle during post-merger integration; the transplant organ gets rejected and shareholders wind up losing a lot of money. Knowing that can happen, I am truly proud of the milestones Data Domain has continued to achieve as part of EMC. Perhaps one of the most important is that 18 months after the acquisition, all our execs were still on the job at EMC.

Chapter 20
A RECIPE for success

So much has been written about company culture. You can't exactly see, smell, or touch "culture," but you can experience it. In business, culture is about values, what we value—and what we don't—as a group of people. I came into the company with an agenda on values. I had found culture sorely lacking as a business asset in the companies where I had worked before: there was too much fear, insecurity, politics, and cronyism. I am neither a moralist nor some sort of enlightened manager— I simply thought that culture could work for us, instead of against us. At minimum, good culture could make Data Domain a more pleasant place to work. That was a value in its own right.

The reality is that with or without you, your company will have a culture. Any time people come together in some organizational context, culture happens. Is your culture helping or hurting the company? I started new-hire induction meetings with the statement that in the 20th century mankind managed to kill tens of millions of people, and we scarcely remember why. It is innate in human nature that when people come together without the right behavioral guidance, they can do very bad things to each other. The last couple millennia of history are ample illustration.

Our drive for a set of values in the organization came about gradually, as more people came into the company. We started writing them down and describing them:

    Respect
    Excellence
    Customer
    Integrity
    Performance
    Execution

The first letter of each of the six values spells the word R-E-C-I-P-E. We did not aim for an acronym of sorts. We put up the list in an All Hands meeting years ago and one of our engineers crowed, "Hey, that spells RECIPE, if you re-order them." Cool, we ran with it—our RECIPE for business success.

Becoming a value-led organization doesn't happen automatically. We imported somebody else's culture with every person we hired, and therefore had to undo a bunch of stuff. We called it "re-programming." People learn culture based on what behavior they observe around them, good, bad, or somewhere in between. Aside from pointed, serious, and explicit communication, these values could only stick if our management team lived by them and forced compliance—people learn best by example. Values are abstract concepts until you have a live situation at hand; situations are an opportunity to drive compliance and demonstrate what you mean.

Virtually every company professes affection for "Respect" or "Respect for the individual," but very few prosecute the violations. Hence, it rings hollow, becoming a running joke, a double standard. People learn behavior based on how an organization reacts to what they see around them. Be aware: just condoning (through "benign neglect") sanctions behavior.

RECIPE was an internal-only framework at first. We were pleasantly surprised by how well employees received this kind of information. There was an unspoken yearning for it, and it helped center us as a group. They wholeheartedly embraced it because, let's face it, it is a lot of motherhood, baseball, and apple pie. How can you disagree with these values? But it's one thing to nod approval to a list of abstract platitudes—that's easy. No teeth. The magic begins when you start displaying what you mean by them in practice, when the consequences are real.

One aspect of compliance was that we told new hires upfront that while we might be somewhat patient and forgiving on performance, we would not be on conduct. Conduct is a choice, not a skill set. If someone made the wrong choices in the face of all the guidance received, it could and would be a dismissible offense. Data Domain was protective of its culture, and if we felt compromised, drastic action was not long in coming. Such action was not a frequent occurrence, but it happened enough to remind folks we were serious about our code of conduct.

RECIPE gradually also found its way outside the organization. This happened naturally, since values deal with not just employees but all your other stakeholders, such as investors, partners, and customers. It was interesting to see how well these parties reacted to us being serious about codifying our own conduct. It set us apart.

I'd go as far as to say that company culture is the only enduring, sustainable form of differentiation. These days, we don't have a monopoly for very long on talent, technology, capital, or any other asset; the one thing that is unique to us is how we choose to come together as a group of people, day in and day out. How many organizations are there that make more than a halfhearted attempt at this?

Once the organization began to align itself and everybody more or less acted on the RECIPE, things changed. There was less friction, less conflict, less politics—at times, things seemed effortless. Communications and processes were short and lightweight: we just understood each other with less effort, and we knew how to come together, and avoid coming apart. A greater and greater portion of the available daily energy was put in the service of our organization (instead of laboring through internal strife, unwanted attrition, too many meetings, warring factions, and other dysfunctions that plague a rudder-less organization).

After some time, an effective culture feeds on itself as a growing part of the organization bought into our RECIPE and reinforces it. I describe each RECIPE ingredient here because I think they are each worth considering. At Data Domain they all became second nature, not something we had to talk about much.

Chapter 21
Respect—the 'R' in RECIPE

Respect goes beyond the customary "we won't discriminate on race, religion, gender, ethnic origin, etc." In any pecking order, favoritism develops. You get inner circles—some of us are on the inside, others not so much. It is invisible and unspoken, but it creates an atmosphere where people spend more time worrying about where they stack up than about their jobs, trying to read the tea leaves all day long. Nice fodder for around the water cooler, but a productivity killer.

We valued respect between managers and employees. We promoted many individual contributors to managers. We emphasized how awesome the responsibility is for other people's work lives. They don't "work for you"—we all work for the company. As a manager, you are there to help them succeed. We put you—the manager—in their service. At Data Domain, managers were evaluated on how good their people were; if we saw any evidence that a manager was exerting unhealthy power behaviors, we got on it.

For example, Data Domain was a company where anybody could talk with anybody, me included. You didn't need your manager's permission to seek somebody out in other parts of the company or "higher up in the chain" (to use another common hierarchical metaphor, like "he works for her"). A lot of managers are insecure this way. Well, do not be that way at Data Domain—if you can't stand the transparency, you are in the wrong place. Gate keeping and trying to control communications internally is something we frowned on. Don't get me wrong: organizations establish standard escalation paths for the sake of efficiency. But individuals better not put their own agenda ahead of the company's—that is unacceptable.

We put emphasis on respect between organizations as much as individuals. The classic case is where sales walk taller than the rest of the organization because they "bring home the bacon," getting to boss everybody else around, especially engineering. Senior management (at companies where I've worked before) often condones this, but at Data Domain we did not. When you hire lots of sales staff, you better get in front of this because chances are they bring these supremacy attitudes with them. Your sales leadership better be simpatico with you, because they are going to need to get behind this on a daily basis, driving compliance by example. We were fortunate that we had the kind of sales leaders who were not loud-mouthed brow beaters, but smart, thoughtful people— requests came with urgency, but not attitude. David Schneider, VP of Sales, embraced this standard of conduct between teams early on, and kept setting the tone in the sales organization for civility between teams.

There are other startup scenarios where engineering staffs are the prima donnas, and that can be equally dysfunctional and detrimental. Data Domain never suffered from that syndrome: our founding technical team was centered on the customer from day one.

A successful startup takes a lot more than a strong sales team; all the pieces need to come together in splendid harmony. We often used to joke that it "takes a village" to make a sale, and it does—everybody is important. We had a respectful partnership between sales and other organizations, and we credited that as part of a successful culture. Engineering has as big a voice as sales. Respect between teams requires trust, judgment, and a unifying vision, starting from the top of the house.

Chapter 22
Excellence—the first 'E' in RECIPE

We fashioned ourselves as a blue-collar company from the start: we wanted to be good at the craft of what we did, whatever it was. A lot of design elegance and fine carpentry are hidden deep within the guts of the best high-tech products. We wanted to build really good products, never just "good enough" products that we could "get away with."

We focused on quality from day one. It can be hard, because quality doesn't expand your addressable market; you feel constantly pressured to make decisions that compromise quality. People tell you quality will slow down releases of new products, cost more, add complexity, or jack up risk. Nevertheless, we wanted our engineers to be vocal about problems that had to be fixed even though (in the immediate sense) it would not land us one more deal. Our customer-support staff was a full partner representing these customer issues to engineering.

Many of us had managed product lines where shortcuts were taken early on, and had lived through the hell of never-ending customer escalations and dissatisfaction. It is not worth it. More strategically, a business scales and grows much faster when the products are rock solid, as the organization is not bogged down by endless quality problems. Salespeople can sell with confidence, create a happy camper, and move on to the next deal; strong references (who voluntarily become your "promoters") are priceless marketing collateral.

It is hard to build momentum on a poorly conceived chassis—the time to commit to unyielding quality focus is early, early, early. Short of a major pit stop, it is quite hard to retrofit the quality once you find yourself hurtling down the track. In hindsight, you see you actually had more bandwidth to do this sooner than later.

Customer satisfaction always affected our notion of "a win." A sales contract is not yet a complete win: the end zone is when we have implemented successfully and created a delighted customer. Not just some revenue, but another brick in the wall of building a company one thrilled customer at a time. Selling a deal was great, but we immediately felt the pressure of making sure that customer was successful. Being blue-collar meant pride in workmanship and full accountability—if we ever fell short, it was a major event to be scrutinized and learned from by all of us. We took everything personally.

The notion of "blue collar" spread to our general conduct. We traveled alone, made few many-legged sales calls, and booked cheap flights and hotels: everybody tried to save a dime for the company. Raising more capital meant equity dilution, and nobody wanted that, of course. Our marketing money was spent as a front-end to sales rather than to see our name in lights at some venue or forum. Speaking of venues, we justified a trade show presence by the number of leads we generated. We knew what leads cost and what they yielded. We rarely did anything to generate "buzz" for its own sake—we put all our resources into building, selling, and supporting products.

Excellence was not just for our products and services. We employed people who were in finance, accounting, HR, legal, and we wanted them to be the best at what they did for us. It is common for people to accept the status quo, capitulate, and have peace with the current standard. We wanted a culture that was perpetually dissatisfied with the status quo. Our glasses were always half empty— there was always room up, on everything. Even when the company became a rocket ship, heads were down, no stupid grins.

Early on, when employee candidates asked us what our culture was like, we invariably said "blue collar." Not a lot of flash—if it doesn't directly aid our cause, we don't spend money on it. Extravagance was frowned upon, and becoming self-congratulatory was avoided; these things weaken the focus and muscle of the company. Setting the tone comes from the top. Humble and hungry is what we wanted to be.

Chapter 23
Customer—the 'C' in RECIPE

We already discussed the value of snuggling up to our customers; taking this to another level, we made it part of Data Domain's culture for people to intuitively act in the best interest of the customer. I don't believe this sits in the category of motherhood and apple pie—there are plenty of companies who explicitly put their employees or investors first. We did not. Customers' ongoing support of our company was our lifeline, oxygen in our tank, and we were not even a business without them. Customers had got us to where we were. We were never confused about that, and would drop everything to help a customer. We put product releases on hold to free up resources for support, refusing to leave customers behind while we were busy acquiring new ones.

We were not just trying to satisfy customers—we were trying to turn them into rabid fans of our people, our products, our services, and our company. When our customer count reached the many hundreds, we implemented the quarterly Net Promoter Score (NPS) Survey to monitor how successful we were in creating fans. Customers were asked how likely (on a scale from 1-10) they were to recommend Data Domain to a friend or a colleague. 9s and 10s were considered "promoters," below 6 they were "detractors," and in between, "passives." To get the Net Promoter Score, subtract detractors from promoters (as a percentage of the total); a score of 0 indicates as many promoters as detractors. Our scores hovered in the low 50s, which is very high for this category of product. The survey also detailed feedback we needed to know to improve our scores.

One of the things we were proudest of was how our employees often took matters into their own hands to help customers, way beyond the call of duty. One of our people once drove a thousand miles in two days to deliver new systems to a customer in Louisiana right before a hurricane was making landfall. They took such ownership of customer success, and it was inspiring for everybody else to hear the stories.

Chapter 24
Integrity—the 'I' in RECIPE

Like respect, integrity is not controversial at first blush, but acting with high integrity is another matter—often meaning acting in what appears to be something other than the best interest of the business. In practice, integrity means we never knowingly speak anything but the truth to our stakeholders. Often there is a fuzzy line, but do not go near it. Sometimes we lie by omission—don't do it. If there is pertinent information, share it.

When people tried to finesse a situation and offer some version of the truth, we asked, "does truth have versions?" If it is in the best interest of our customer, partner, or investor to know, we must share that information. This approach didn't always ingratiate me with salespeople or partners—if I thought a customer would not be best served with our solution, I'd say so even though a sale could be sacrificed in the process.

I remember one specific sales situation I was brought into to help a deal along, but instead, I ended up nixing the deal with my assessment. I could see the salesperson and reseller think, "And you are the CEO of this company?" But then the customer started identifying opportunities where we might be a good fit in future—he had started trusting us to recommend the right product. It doesn't always work out that way, though, which makes it hard to maintain your resolve. Opting out usually happened when we pursued a poorly qualified opportunity where we should not have been in the first place.

Our sales engineers (SEs) were tasked with configuring and sizing systems that fit the customer's needs as best we understood them, and were also responsible post-sale to help install and implement. We held them accountable for customer success. They were teamed directly with a sales account lead, and served as a check on overzealous sales promises (since they had to make good on them). Customers would often complain that we were expensive, but once they did the apples-to-apples comparison, we weren't nearly as pricey as they thought: the competition was notorious for under-sizing the system to appear more competitive. When the customer later complained, they would just make it up to them with additional gear. That was not our way.

How did this all help our cause? Integrity engenders trust, which is arguably the most priceless currency in business (and in any other human endeavor, for that matter). Stephen Covey, Jr. wrote a terrific book titled *The Speed of Trust* about this—when people trust you, they hand their business to you with their eyes closed. Trust makes business just go, because customers know you have their back. The opposite is also true: lack of trust becomes an inhibitor to business. Trust is good for business. How do you earn trust? Act with high integrity.

When it comes to employees, being truthful can be equally challenging because no one wants to deliver negative news. Here, too, draw a line in the sand. We always shared the exact same materials with our employees as we did with our board (of course, once you go public, you cannot do that, in view of SEC regulations). When questions came—and our employees were not shy—we answered them. If I could not publicly answer the question, and I would just say so, rather than fabricate an answer to appease the questioner. The more direct you are in answering questions, the more people are inclined to take you for your word. It is not a small thing in this day and age for employees to actually trust their management.

Before we went public we would often share, informally, our revenue and sales information with industry analysts; once we went public, we actually had to disclose the same information in SEC filings. One analyst was blown away that what we told them pre-IPO turned out to be exactly the same as our officially reported numbers. They were so used to being lied to, they discounted whatever they were told by a huge factor. It changed our relationship: they started trusting us. We could have spun and fabricated data, but we didn't.

I already covered our attitude toward the board of directors, namely transparency and intellectual honesty, and hence, trust. Once public, we were equally upfront with the capital markets in our quarterly calls. It kept us out of trouble. Do not pick and choose where you will and won't apply the standard of integrity—trust is hard to gain and easy to lose, so let your word be your bond.

Chapter 25
Performance—the 'P' in RECIPE

Discrimination was of course undesirable, and we did not discriminate on personal attributes, save one: performance. We hired, fired, promoted, rewarded, and recognized based on performance. It doesn't matter whom you knew or what school or club you belonged to, and you could have green hair, tattoos, piercings, etc., for all we cared—what mattered was what you contributed to the company. This is not just fair, it also helps everyone succeed as a business. Not much should get in the way of a performance culture; every incentive and behavior must help elevate performance.

Like with all our values, we tried to be upfront with people and manage personal performance aggressively. Be a driver, which we need, not simply a passenger on the ship, which we cannot afford on this leg of the journey. Passengers are ballast, cargo, deadweight freight—they are a resource sink, yet they end up in the same destination as the drivers. That is not right. If you're not sure what you are, find out: do not be passive. Somebody once asked me how he or she would know whether they were a driver, and I answered, "you better find out before we do." In other words, be more demanding of yourself. Are you increasing the company's speed or not?

Performance was also central to our compensation, and all our execs (not just sales) had sales-like compensation plans. We had no Management-By-Objectives (MBO) goal setting, and wanted all executives paid on the same metric: growth of the business. We had hurdles on profitability, but the goal was growth, and growth only. No dilution of focus. We had to wrestle the board on this every year, because it was natural for them to want a more balanced set of goals. But balance can mean dilution of focus, and if you stop growing as a startup, your days are numbered as an independent company. A startup sometimes feels like rodeo—see if you can hang on for the 8-second ride before getting bucked off. There is no balanced scorecard in rodeo.

Later on when we became profitable, we instituted bonus pools for rank-and-file employees; they did not get MBOs either. We allocated bonus money to departments and asked the managers to allocate that money every quarter and produce a strong bell curve where the smallest bonus was 0% and the largest was 200-300%. It forced managers to stack-rank their employees every quarter. If they wanted to shower their top talent with more money, they had to take it from the ones not in good standing — no peanut butter spread where everybody gets 100% of his or her bonus. That is entitlement, a bad word in our culture. Moreover, they had to have conversations with all these employees as to why they got what they got. Once this becomes part of the culture, it is amazingly easy to do. It also takes HR out of the process, making it a manager's job to manage performance.

Data Domain Human Resources, led by Shelly Begun, used this "calibration system" to support our managerial staff with performance management. If we had to part ways with an employee, we expected to see a pattern of sub-par bonuses in the preceding quarters. It is much harder to settle a separation when the employee in question has been paid a full bonus every quarter—how would they know they weren't doing well? Often, employees would leave voluntarily after a few quarters of sub-par bonuses; they had internalized the message and taken action. As an organization, we were getting the desired behavior: either step up, or step out. This may sound harsh, but you owe it to the other 95% or so of your employees— another test of your leadership.

Chapter 26
Execution—the second 'E' in RECIPE

We were big on execution, which is a close corollary to the Excellence in RECIPE. In early-stage ventures, companies often spend more time on strategy than execution, always second-guessing themselves. Did we have the right strategy for product, for channel, for go-to-market? It is easy to lose resolve, always chasing the mythical strategy that will leave everybody in the dust. Early on, the feedback from the market is murky—it's easy to get discouraged.

You can't know whether your strategy is any good until you are executing it well; therefore, you might as well shift focus from strategy to execution. Put differently, no strategy is better than its execution. When you get better at execution, the strategic issues will crystallize more as well.

Changing strategy frequently is akin to planting a seedling and pulling it out of the ground every day to see if it is growing yet—you need to give a strategy time and nurturing before deciding that it is in need of revision. In the startup combat zone, we felt that instead of revisiting our strategy at the first sign of trouble, we would instead double down on our strategy commitment. The watchword was heads down execution, one foot in front of the other, addressing the details of the business as best we knew how.

We saw our competition constantly shift strategy, with a new message for the analysts every six months—a sign of leadership in crisis. Of course, our relentless execution caused them to lose heart even more. Lurching left and right confuses customers, and employees wonder whether you know what you're doing. By the time we looked up from our heads-down position, we had pulled way out in front of the competition. Like art being 99% perspiration (versus inspiration), business is 99% execution (versus strategy). A company can go a long way with an average strategy and superior execution, but they will not go far without great execution, no matter how brilliant the strategy.

I consider myself a student of both strategy and execution, and occasionally I'm tempted to claim I rolled out a grand strategy for Data Domain. But that just isn't how it happened. Data Domain's strategy was more or less in place by the time I joined the company—if I did anything right, it was that I didn't mess with that strategy over the next seven years.

Chapter 27
Did RECIPE survive?

There is no finessing this question. EMC and Data Domain were quite different. Although they were both sales-oriented companies and Data Domain had hired many former EMC sales staff, we differed in most other ways. We quipped that maybe we could perform "stem cell therapy" with our culture on the much larger organism of EMC—and in some ways, we did.

Joe Tucci was quite taken, for example, with our Net Promoter Score Survey methodology and introduced it EMC-wide. Our "performance calibration" system raised tons of eyebrows because EMC was big on MBOs. The standard put-down was that our methods were "very nice" but "would not scale." But we moved 1,500 employees we inherited from other parts of EMC to the system inside one quarter, without a hitch—apparently, it scaled fine, MBOs be damned.

Still, we grew to learn that our respective cultures were opposites. The EMC bureaucracy would not yield to Data Domain. Who did we think we were? That said, Data Domain was the largest acquisition ever attempted by EMC, and EMC executives were rightfully protecting the new asset against silly, petty politics by the home office.

Our HR team used personality-profiling methods to help us better understand our own behavioral tendencies. Data Domain executives were birds of a feather; most of us clustered on key criteria. After the merger, we profiled the EMC leaders coming over to our organization to see how they would fit. The comparison was an eye-opener, to say the least, and it helped us gain insight into the cultural divide between the companies.

For example, former Data Domain execs were mostly so-called "low socials." They don't value relationships per se; they value what people bring to the business instead. Data Domain people did not hang out together after work much—we served in the same war together, but that was it. EMC executives, on the other hand, were "high socials." EMC has a relationship culture that functions on whom you know. It is a 30-year-old company, so senior staff have a lot of continuity and years in the company. EMC people solve for career longevity, while Data Domain people just wanted the doors to be open the next day.

Data Domain execs are also characterized as "low compliance and high asserts," meaning that they do not fall in line easily if they disagree, and they speak their minds no matter who is in the room. At EMC—a very large company—people survived by being the inverse: "high compliance and low asserts." Data Domain people questioned the ways EMC did things, and were called "righteous" by some of the EMC bureaucracy. They did not intend that as a compliment.

Yet even within EMC, I can see that RECIPE will live on in the hearts and minds of Data Domain people. And this will continue to pay off for EMC shareholders over the long haul.

Chapter 28
What's it like?

Startups are a crapshoot, and the odds for a billion-dollar exit are exceedingly small. Being part of one in your life is a true privilege—being its CEO is a winning lottery ticket. We have to get lucky. We keep reminding ourselves that no matter how well we may have played our cards, we started the game with a very good hand. Even when that wasn't readily apparent at the time, it sure is in hindsight.

With their relentless pace and pressure, startups are not for everybody. The fluidity, the lack of structure and process—it is business in its rawest form. There is nowhere to hide.

Startup CEOs are more like plow horses than racehorses. A racehorse gets pampered all week, to be taken out of the barn for a few minutes to race on Saturday afternoon; startup CEOs live 12+ hours a day behind the plow. It doesn't feel so glamorous when you get home at 11 at night and you need to get up at 5 am to catch a flight out of town.

Coming from bigger companies, I found the startup experience exhilarating and liberating. Like sailing a dinghy: direct feedback all the time, close to the metal. It's heady, like breathing pure oxygen. Many constraints but few limits.

On weekends I sometimes competed in middle-distance triathlons and marathons, and people wondered how I made time for that. The truth is, I needed it to maintain perspective and clarity of thought—physical health, yes, but even more so, mental health. You rarely get more focused, uninterrupted thinking time than when you are on a run or on a bike for hours on end. The sport also helped steel me mentally for business. Triathlon is racing at near-redline exertion for long periods of time, so you need to find a way to sustain high levels of effort without burning yourself up and to endure increasing levels of discomfort first, and later, sheer pain. That is familiar terrain for a startup CEO.

Being acquired by EMC was challenging for such a fiercely independent company as Data Domain, and EMC is a great company. Once the deal went through, though, we felt much like a guest in our own house. It is hard to go back into the "Matrix" once one has been in the startup life!

So, enjoy the ride—those 8 seconds can become the most meaningful time in your work life!

Frank Slootman
Los Gatos, California
Fslootman@me.com

About the Author

Frank Slootman served as President and Chief Executive Officer (CEO) from mid-2003 through the acquisition of the company in the summer of 2009. Prior to Data Domain, Frank held executive technology management roles at Borland and Compuware Corporation. A native from The Netherlands, Frank started his career with Burroughs Corporation in Detroit. Today, Frank is the Chief Executive Officer of Service-now.com in San Diego.

14710404R00064

Made in the USA
San Bernardino, CA
02 September 2014